I0164510

To those who understand
the value of
sex education that
protects us from
unrealistic expectations

Understanding

Sexual Response

ISBN 978-0956894-762

Published by *Nosper Books* 2021

Copyright © Jane Thomas 2021

www.nosper.com

Contents

I   An evidence-based approach to researching sexuality

I am documenting my research approach, which is different to that taken by other researchers. I have not had a budget, colleagues or the support of an academic institution to engage in the kind of research that has been done in the past. My sex research is based on a much more basic assumption.

I set out on a quest to find evidence for the orgasms, women are presumed to have with a lover. As a woman who has never experienced even one of these, I decided to approach other women in the population (face-to-face or via the internet) and ask them to explain how they achieve orgasm. So I ask women to explain the erotic turn-ons that cause their mental arousal. I also ask them to describe the stimulation technique they use to orgasm.

This is my research. Some people might say that this approach is unscientific because it does not involve wearing a lab coat or having qualifications in sexology. I am asking why these credentials matter. If women were truly having orgasms, they would know these basic facts. Surely, at least some of them would be able to explain the anomalies and contradictions in the popular beliefs that I am highlighting? Equally, if women enjoyed sexual pleasuring, they would be willing to talk about it. That is my science.

Understanding sexual response involves challenging popular beliefs as well as comparing and contrasting male and female sexuality. I have organised my search for answers into the following three categories:

- Identifying the misconceptions and erroneous assumptions
- Establishing similarities between male and female responsiveness
- Explaining the differences between male and female responses

I spent years trying to understand my sexuality in the light of the apparent evidence from erotic fiction. Luckily, I love the intellectual challenge of unchartered territory. Kinsey and Hite's findings were the only hint that my experiences were not unique. I questioned everything I assumed to be true. I invited others via the internet to suggest how women enjoy sexual pleasure. Few people have had anything significant to say. I wondered about all the silence and I have even drawn my own conclusions from it.

In any scientific endeavour, however, evidence is vital.[1] So I present the biological precedents for sexuality. I provide an interpretation of the research findings. I compare men and women's behaviours in sexual scenarios. I discuss sexual response in sufficient detail to help others appreciate the issues. I cite other researchers and women in the general population.

II   Identifying the erroneous assumptions about sexuality

We tend to assume (on the basis of erotic fiction) that women in real life:

- Have the exact same sexual needs that men have;
- Respond to real-world erotic triggers as men do;
- Experience arousal and orgasm as easily as men do;
- Are driven to engage in intercourse just as men are;
- Masturbate as commonly and as frequently as men;
- Can masturbate themselves to orgasm with a lover;
- Orgasm from vaginal stimulation (intercourse);
- Orgasm from clitoral stimulation (cunnilingus);
- Are constantly aroused and orgasmic with a lover; and
- Are proactive lovers due to their own arousal.

It has taken years for me to reach my current conclusions. Like everyone else, I was handicapped by assumptions based on popular beliefs about sexuality as portrayed in pornography and erotic fiction. This sexual ignorance is not backed by any conclusive research findings but it is reinforced by the society around us, both in our private lives as well as in magazines or in movies. This is natural, given the lack of authoritative sex education.

Anyone who researches sexuality makes the same assumptions and has the same misunderstandings we all do. For a long time, I didn't even realise the need to challenge these misconceptions. They are so universal that they are never doubted. Men assume, due to their own experience, that women are just as easily aroused and capable of orgasm as they are. Women profit from the attention and the money to be made out of promoting fantasies.

My research started with my own experiences of sex and masturbation. I then used Shere Hite's work and Alfred Kinsey's to understand how my own sexuality fitted with their conclusions. They had relied on the assumption that every woman knows what an orgasm is. Whereas my work differentiates between sexual responsiveness (our subconscious ability to respond to eroticism) and conscious behaviours aimed at pleasing a lover.

Over time I have come to realise that my work is not about science as such because science implies discovering something new. My work involves applying basic common sense. I ask questions that reveal truths. I question assumptions. Very few people appear to see the need to do this. Not only are they reassured by beliefs that are not founded in any kind of facts or logic but they are extremely unwilling to have those beliefs challenged.[2]

2.1 Women have the exact same sexual needs that men have

Sex research appears to indicate that many women orgasm both alone and with a lover. But all of this research is flawed because there is no agreement on what physical and mental stimuli cause women to experience orgasm. Erotic fiction shows women apparently having orgasms from whatever stimulation their lovers choose to provide. So while male orgasm clearly depends on stimulation focused on the penis, it is assumed that women orgasm from almost any stimulation of any body part that a lover chooses to stimulate for them. There is no consistency between women's orgasm techniques either alone, with a man or with another woman. While male erotic turn-ons are clearly defined and well-known, no one can name even one female erotic turn-on that might cause their arousal with a lover.

Women who advise the public on female orgasm never support their theories with evidence from their own experiences. They promote textbook theories about women's presumed experiences. They are reassured by women in the population who are easily pressured into believing that they should respond to the stimulation men provide.[3] Women, with doctorates and professional qualifications in sexology, talk from a script (like porn stars) that has been prepared for them (probably by a man). It is highly irresponsible to promote male fantasies that no one can explain logically.

Why is porn so popular if it reflects so accurately the responsiveness, proactiveness and enthusiasm for sex that women have in real life? Men honestly seem to believe that female porn stars are truly aroused on screen and having orgasms, not just acting. Obviously, excellent acting…! My work on sexuality is aimed at opening up the topic. I provide a constructive discussion of arousal and orgasm for those who know what I am talking about. But I have never found any other couples who can suggest sexual techniques for pleasuring women. Intercourse defines even lesbian's sex lives (tribbing involves emulating heterosexual coitus without the penetration). The silence is due to the gap between erotic fiction and the reality.

For most couples, intercourse defines their sex life from start to finish. The inherent conclusion must be that intercourse is just as sexually rewarding for women as it is for men. Yet women do not talk of intercourse as a crude act of sexual gratification. They talk of lovemaking. Both heterosexual and lesbian women focus their appreciation of lovemaking (intercourse or other activities) on the closeness (emotional intimacy) and touching (sensual pleasure) involved in physical intimacy with a loving partner. Women rarely refer explicitly to sexual anatomy or genital stimulation with a lover.

2.1.1 Women respond to real-world erotic triggers as men do

Men are aroused by nudity and sexual opportunities, so it is assumed that women are too. The fact that pornography is censored in every society is ignored. No one seems to notice that women do not ogle anyone's genitals. Women consider genitals to be ugly and smelly parts of the body. My own experience is that I am not aroused by genitals in reality (but neither am I disgusted by them). But when I masturbate alone, I need to use explicitly erotic concepts based on penetrative sex in order to achieve orgasm. For me, sexual pleasure is about enjoying my brain's response to eroticism.

Once I was invited to attend a sex fair with a couple of women who ran a sex toy business. They explained that they only sold toys. They had chosen not to sell erotic material such as erotic books and movies. They said that their female customers considered erotic material to be obscene.[4] Sex toys are acceptable to women because they are functional gadgets without erotic significance (except perhaps those huge black phalluses one sees!).

I have found this reaction to be typical of women. They justify sex in terms of a loving relationship and having a family through a committed relationship. A woman is known to engage in sex because she is married. The fact is implicit because of her legal commitment to a relationship with a man. But she never refers explicitly to sexual activity. Neither does she admire male genitals or male responses. This is in stark contrast to men, who lust after women's bodies and refer explicitly to every aspect of sexual activity.

The penis must be rigid before a man can orgasm. This is a prerequisite of male orgasm. A man's erection comes from what is happening in his mind. His mind or senses (sight, smell etc) respond to erotic stimuli that cause the nervous excitement we call arousal. This same process must logically also occur for women if they are to experience orgasm. Responsive women use a much more complex mechanism to become aroused. But unfortunately this mechanism only works when a woman is alone. If women were aroused with a lover, they would be able to explain their turn-ons. Women in the general population would be able to explain how they get aroused.

Women use the word eroticism without having the least idea what this means to men. They think that any activity that includes nudity is erotic. So they take their clothes off and the scenario is erotic. But sex is erotic from the perspective of the penetrating male, who has the opportunity to obtain his sexual release through thrusting. It is not erotic from the perspective of the receiver. Whether a woman offers her mouth, her vagina or her anus, she is offering a man an opportunity to ejaculate into her body.

2.1.2 Women experience arousal and orgasm as easily as men do

Kinsey noted that women who could masturbate to orgasm said they also had orgasms with a lover. This is contrary to my experience. I wonder whether women who think that they orgasm with a lover (which is quite impossible) also think that they orgasm when masturbating because they assume that almost any stimulation causes orgasm (as portrayed in erotic fiction). Incredible though it seems, they are mistaken in both situations. Two biological precedents should cause us to question beliefs about female orgasm. Homo sapiens evolved from more primitive mammals. There is no evidence that female mammals ever orgasm. Also male orgasm triggers the reproductive process but female orgasm is not required at all.

I ask women on the internet every day to explain how they enjoy eroticism, sexual pleasure and orgasm. Specifically I ask them to account for their arousal with a lover. I ask them to specify the erotic turn-ons that cause their arousal. I also ask them to explain the anatomy and the stimulation technique that they use to reach orgasm. Silence reigns.[5] Women assume that intercourse is supposed to provide their sexual pleasure. This is because men assume that the receiver of intercourse must obtain the same satisfaction as the penetrating male. But no one can explain how a woman can achieve orgasm from stimulation that lasts for a random length of time.

Women are never asked to explain how they are aroused. Researchers do not take human psychology into account. When asked questions, we do not always have answers but we may feel obliged to provide an answer. Most women never respond positively to eroticism. Women talk of being aroused with no idea of what men experience. They assume that their willingness to allow a man to ejaculate into their vagina equates to arousal. They assume that they are aroused and have orgasms because they engage in intercourse. But intercourse is arousing from the perspective of the penetrating male because he needs an erection to engage in it. For a woman, intercourse is just a matter of remaining in position until a man ejaculates.

Whenever anyone (a man or a woman) stimulates a woman sexually, they tend to stimulate a variety of anatomy. Stimulation is directed to every part of the female body because women rarely communicate a preference. This is a clear indication that women are not aroused with a lover. So when researchers ask women about the anatomy involved in their presumed orgasms, women agree to whatever anatomy is suggested to them. Typically, more informed women opt for clitoral stimulation, while less educated women continue to suggest that they orgasm from vaginal stimulation.

2.1.3 Women are driven to engage in intercourse just as men are

Men have a drive to obtain intercourse that we see throughout Nature. We observe the male of the species being motivated to mate with a female. In an attempt to establish political equality, feminists assert that women have a sex drive to engage in activity that potentially impregnates them. Libido encapsulates the idea that women have a choice over intercourse. Women's amenability depends on emotional factors. Yet sex drive is biological. Men observe that young women offer sex more readily than older women. But women's desire for family has nothing to do with a sex drive.

The most fundamental belief anyone has about female orgasm is that it should occur from intercourse. But the precise mechanism that causes female orgasm and the timing of a woman's orgasm is never specified. Women are supposed to orgasm at some point before intercourse ends. Alfred Kinsey found that a woman's presumed enthusiasm for intercourse (based on orgasm claims) had no impact on intercourse frequencies.[6] Shere Hite found that women valued closeness and touching more than orgasm.

While talking to Silvia, an older woman I have known for years, I referred to my work. Her angry reply alienated me: "There's nothing wrong with my sexuality!". The inference was that she enjoyed intercourse as normal women are meant to. Whereas I engaged in clitoral stimulation and fantasies, which women consider obscene. The discussion was evidently over. How could anyone believe that such a dismissive response indicates that a woman enjoys sexual pleasure or that she knows anything about orgasm?

My experience of women who comment on sex is that they are only interested in the topic to the extent that they can reassure themselves, and no doubt others, that they are 'sexually normal' as defined by our society. They never give any explicit details and they certainly have no friendly advice for a woman, like myself, who questions the feasibility of these orgasms they are presumed to enjoy (not explicitly but inherently because they engage in intercourse). By conforming to the beliefs in the society around them, they avoid conflict and obtain reassurance and acceptance.

There are many references to women's disappointment with sex in the popular media. Why are these experiences women have openly referred to and yet still remain unacknowledged? I have concluded that the explanations are too unpopular. Women always use euphemisms to talk about intercourse. Sex seems to be just a life experience that every woman is expected to acquire by a certain age. The universal promotion of erotic fiction and the lack of a more realistic picture mean that we cannot accept the reality.

2.2 Women masturbate as commonly and as frequently as men

Most men masturbate at least when they are adolescent so they assume that women must have a similar experience. Men never seem to notice that women do not welcome images of male genitals nor are they willing to watch portrayals of sexual activity. Women never refer to the erotic turn-ons that might cause their arousal nor can they specify the anatomy involved in orgasm. Contrary to popular beliefs, female masturbation and orgasm are rare. Female responsiveness is presumably the result of a recessive gene. Perhaps it is a random genetic characteristic that affects very few women and can be compared with the one that causes homosexuality.

Female responsiveness is difficult to estimate given its highly sporadic nature. I masturbate for a few days in a row, often morning and evening. Then I don't masturbate for weeks. Kinsey found women masturbated to orgasm on average once every 2 to 3 weeks. My averages (based on my memory) are not so different to this finding, which is an amazing coincidence because his statistics included women who masturbate without ever achieving orgasm. The overall orgasm frequencies for women, including those who mistake with a lover, were higher than those for masturbation.[7]

The research into female orgasm, clearly indicates that women are much more confident of achieving orgasm when they are alone. The reasons for this are never explained. My own explanation includes:

- Responsiveness depends on the brain responding to eroticism.
- Women have little conscious awareness of erotic arousal.
- Very few women are responsive enough to discover orgasm.
- Orgasm is a vital aspect of male reproductive function.
- Women are only capable of orgasm because they have a phallus.
- Women are rarely consciously aware of the internal clitoral organ.
- Responsive women use surreal fantasy to generate erotic arousal.
- To obtain the intensity of mental focus a woman must be alone.
- The instinctive stimulation is incompatible with sociable activity.

Kinsey's work was ignored for a number of reasons. He provided considerable evidence to show that female orgasm is associated with masturbation alone. Kinsey talked about sexual activity explicitly, which is shocking to many people (especially women). Finally, no one was willing to accept Kinsey's conclusion that women are much less responsive than men. The belief in female orgasm justifies women's participation in sexual activity that pleasures men. But also women want to be attractive to men.

7

2.2.1 Women can masturbate themselves to orgasm with a lover

Pornography shows women masturbating (or being masturbated by a lover). This self-stimulation by fingering around their glans never ends in orgasm. Women are shown continuing to engage in sexual activity after masturbating so orgasm is clearly not their goal. Despite the publication of Hite's findings that women are more successful with orgasm alone, heterosexuals continue to assume that the vagina is the focus of women's pleasure. Heterosexuals have never had any real interest in the clitoris. They are unimpressed by the endless promotion of the clitoris by sex educators and the indisputable anatomical evidence that the clitoris is the organ equivalent to the penis. Both Alfred Kinsey and Shere Hite found that women are more successful in reaching orgasm when they are alone. But they could not explain why the same orgasm techniques did not work with a partner.[8]

One issue is that the precise anatomy and the stimulation technique involved in female masturbation are never specified. Few women discover how to achieve arousal so they simply guess which anatomy should be stimulated and assume that they orgasm from this stimulation. Given their role as the receiver in intercourse, some women assume they are supposed to stimulate the vagina. This misunderstanding is exacerbated because many sex toys are in the form of a phallus. No one explains which part of the clitoral organ is stimulated. Most people assume it must be the glans (the only visible part of the organ). Yet the glans lacks the erectile tissue (corpora cavernosa) of the shaft of the penis and the internal clitoral organ.

Another issue is that women's psychological arousal is not considered necessary to achieve orgasm. Male erotic turn-ons are specific and well-documented but no one can name any female erotic turn-ons. Sex toys can be marketed as a means of solving women's orgasm problems because women never appreciate the need for erotic arousal. This is because very few women have sufficient responsiveness to achieve orgasm even alone.

I question whether women stimulate themselves to orgasm with a lover. If they do, why are heterosexuals so unaware of the role of the clitoris? Most men (often the less educated) do not need erotic turn-ons. They focus on intercourse. Others want to enjoy their own arousal by focusing on turn-ons. But men focus stimulation on the anatomy that arouses them. Porno orgasms (those men assume women should have with a lover) involve different anatomy because men provide all the stimulation of a sexual encounter. Women are sexually passive with a lover due to lack of arousal. It took me years to work through the logic that enabled me to explain this.

2.2.2 Women orgasm from vaginal stimulation (intercourse)

Kinsey explained that the vagina evolved from primitive egg ducts, which lack any sensitivity (in common with other internal organs of the body). The vagina is the result of glands that develop in the female foetus but not in the male. Just as the male glands (including the prostate) develop in the male foetus but not in the female. Both sets of glands produce the reproductive anatomy of the sexes. There is no logic to suggesting that men and women have evolved different anatomy capable of producing an orgasm.

Intercourse is an act that a man initiates when he has an erection. A woman simply accepts or rejects his offer to thrust into her vagina. A man assumes that a woman feels the same pleasure from the thrusting action of intercourse that he enjoys. But a woman only accepts a male lover after he has proven himself to be a worthy mate, by being affectionate, companionable, caring and supportive. She is reassured by his sexual admiration, which she hopes will incentivise him to support her and a family over decades.

I have described my experiences in as much scientific detail as possible. They do not conform to any popularised account of women's sexuality. More importantly, my experience does not reflect male fantasies. Intercourse is core to male sexuality so it is assumed to be the same for women. But I cannot find anyone, even a so-called professional, who can explain my experiences in a way that is logical and factual. Typically I am met with silence or I am told that there is something undefined wrong with me that cannot be explained scientifically. I also question the angry and defensive response that I get. Why are people, who are supposedly so sure of their opinions, so incapable of explaining or supporting their beliefs?

Everyone is so accustomed to the fiction that no one recognises a woman's real experiences when they hear them.[9] If a woman ever complains about the tedium of intercourse, no one is sympathetic. Even women themselves have little sympathy because they assume that it is a woman's duty to provide regular intercourse within a committed relationship. Marriage is based on a man's willingness to support children in return for regular intercourse, so women cannot easily question this implicit trade. My motivation for discussing my experiences is to highlight women's true responses. Other women never do this because it is so unpopular. Men like to discuss their own enjoyment of eroticism and sexual pleasure with a lover. They are also confident to assert that women achieve orgasm with a lover. But they cannot explain any of the specifics of female arousal and orgasm. Essentially, men believe everything that they see in pornography.

2.2.3 Women orgasm from clitoral stimulation (cunnilingus)

Sexologists assume (as we all do) that women should orgasm in all the same scenarios that men do. These are (1) masturbation alone (the female anatomy and stimulation technique are never specified) (2) vaginal intercourse (3) manual stimulation of the clitoral glans with a lover (by herself or her lover) and (4) cunnilingus (oral stimulation of the clitoral glans).

For men, all of these activities (intercourse, fellatio and masturbation) involve stimulating the penis. The stimulation technique is consistent. The shaft of the penis is massaged in a continuous, rhythmic motion. For women, the anatomy varies in each scenario. In intercourse, women are assumed to orgasm from being on the receiving end of male thrusting (women assume a receiving role). A woman is assumed to obtain the necessary stimulation for orgasm from the penis thrusting into her vagina. In foreplay activities, the clitoris is stimulated as if it was a penis. Cunnilingus involves a woman assuming a penetrator role. But women clearly enjoy only sensual pleasure because they talk of hours rather than minutes.[10]

Fellatio involves massaging the corpora cavernosa within the shaft of the penis. Cunnilingus stimulates the glans (the only visible part of the clitoral organ). But the corpora cavernosa are within the shaft of the clitoral organ (inside a woman's body) – not within the glans. Fellatio mimics the male role in intercourse, where the penis penetrates a warm and wet environment. But the glans of the clitoris was never designed to penetrate a vagina.

Once in my twenties, my partner gave me great oral sex. The feelings were good and I thought that maybe I had had an orgasm. Years later I realised I was wrong. I always knew that it was nothing like an orgasm I have from masturbation. For a start, I felt no erotic arousal. But also there was no sense of sexual release. There was no increase in breathing or sense of relaxation afterwards. So why did I think it was an orgasm? Since teenage years, I had read erotic fiction that promoted the fantasy that women routinely orgasm with a lover through intercourse and cunnilingus. So as soon as I felt the slightest twinge, I thought that maybe it was one of the orgasms everyone talks about. This may explain how women mistake orgasm with a lover, especially women who never discover orgasm by masturbating.

Only around 40% of the more than 3,000 women in Shere Hite's sample said that clitoral stimulation (manual or oral) caused orgasm with a lover. Hite could not explain why clitoral stimulation was much less reliable with a lover than when women were alone. Hite, in common with other researchers, ignored the issue of how women achieve psychological arousal.

2.3 Women are constantly aroused and orgasmic with a lover

People are amazed when I question the orgasms actresses are portrayed as having in pornography. They cannot believe that anyone would doubt the fiction. Yet porn is clearly a male masturbation tool. Pornography involves portraying male fantasies that help men reach orgasm when they masturbate alone. Nevertheless, sexologists seem to think that porn is a reasonable starting point for their beliefs about how real women achieve orgasm.

No one thinks it an odd coincidence that male fantasies should define the reality of female responsiveness so precisely. Yet the basis for so-called scientific study is the assumption that real women should respond exactly as the female porn stars and as the women in erotic fiction do. I call them porno orgasms because they only exist in erotic fiction. Opinions on women's sexuality are not called theories because of the convincing evidence from erotic fiction. Neither do sexologists ask women in the population to confirm their theories. Society just ignores any research indicating that real women behave differently to the actresses in pornography.[11]

Kinsey found that women take 10 to 20 minutes or longer to orgasm with a lover. He did not specify the stimulation technique being used, presumably every possible one. This timeframe is close to the time I would estimate for having a climax from anal intercourse or vaginal fisting. Kinsey noted that men orgasm through thrusting within an average of 2 minutes. So they are not thrusting for 20 minutes into a vagina. I suspect the 10 to 20 minutes or longer timeframe comes from the time men are willing to invest in stimulating a woman before they want to thrust to their own orgasm. I don't believe women orgasm by any means with a lover. I always knew what an orgasm was and so I have always known that it does not occur with a lover. Other women appear to have no idea what is involved.

Boys learn that women do not refer to sex nor do they respond positively to sexual references. So men avoid asking their female partners about orgasm. Women have no answers anyway when it comes to their arousal and orgasm. But equally men prefer women's silence to the explanations provided by the research. So the taboo over sex is a combination of women's defensive silence and men's political move to ignore women's antipathy. Sex research has been done. But it has been universally ignored by women as well as by men. It's not just women's sexuality that is distorted by erotic fiction. Men are also shown with never-ending erections and engaging in a range of sexual activities without being obliged to ejaculate. Yet no one seems to see the harm in this belief that reality is the same as erotic fiction.

2.3.1 Women are proactive lovers due to their own arousal

We often hear sex educators blaming men for ignoring women's presumed sexual needs. But why are women so incapable of obtaining their own sexual satisfaction? Why are men responsible for defining women's pleasure? In porn we see women pleasuring a lover and, in turn, being pleasured. The pleasuring appears to be mutual. But while male pleasure focuses on stimulating the penis, women accept men stimulating a variety of anatomy. In fact women are passive receivers[12] of the stimulation men want to provide. Women are passive due to lack of arousal. This is why women cannot suggest any consistent or reliable female orgasm techniques with a lover.

Sex is taboo because of the differences between personal experiences. This is especially true between the sexes. But also orientation is a factor that people find difficult to accept. Heterosexual men cannot understand how gay men are not aroused by women's bodies. Women cannot understand why men are so fascinated with genitals and so obsessed with having sex. Sex is done to women. It does not originate from their own responses. So it is highly embarrassing for most women. Men learn from a young age that sex is a topic that is not mentioned in front of women. So many women are offended even by the mention of the word. This reaction comes from male pressure on women to engage in sexual activity that is primarily for the male's benefit. This makes sex a difficult subject for anyone to discuss.

Men do not eulogise about their own orgasm because it ends their ability to engage in sexual activity. But the concept of female orgasm was equated to the total sexual pleasure a woman could ever hope to experience. Both sexes could use the belief in female orgasm as a means of making their lover feel inadequate. Faking orgasm became a conscious behaviour any woman could use to please a lover. The concept of female orgasm justifies women's participation in activity that, in truth, focuses on male pleasure.

When I first started on my research on the internet, I set up a web-based forum and invited the general public to comment on my articles. Very few people ever did. Most of the comments made were superficial. A tiny number (made by men) had any substance. I had thought other couples might be willing to share their experiences of adventurous sex play. I was wrong. I assumed that men explore women's bodies and that women give feedback as I did. This is evidently not the case. I have concluded that the vast majority of couples have sex lives that are defined by intercourse. This basic mating activity satisfies a man's need for sexual release and involves the woman in minimal effort so that it is relatively trivial for her to offer.

2.3.2 The function of foreplay is to assist with female arousal

Men are proactive lovers because of their arousal. Men enjoy exploring women's bodies because it is arousing for them. Foreplay existed well before any knowledge of the clitoris. A woman allows a man to stimulate her to the boundaries of her sense of propriety. I was just as passive with a lover as any other woman. The only activities I could consciously decide to engage on involved pleasuring my partner. I had no idea what I could do to achieve erotic arousal with a lover. My masturbation technique, of using surreal fantasies alone, was not suitable for use in a social scenario.

In pornography we see a fair amount of foreplay. Both partners are proactive about offering to pleasure their lover. But these scenarios are more like a group sex scenario that a man might pay for, than anyone's sex life. They are based on a scenario where a woman is being paid to provide sexual services for men. In our own sex lives, we might have these pornographic scenarios in our heads as a model but we don't act out similar scenarios for long. They tend to be at the beginning of relationships when couples explore. Women may feel that they would orgasm if foreplay was offered but they are not motivated to ask a partner to supply it. Sex becomes an activity that is initiated by a man to satisfy his immediate needs.

It has always been clear to me that men can enjoy a woman's body in anticipation of thrusting into her vagina until they ejaculate, which is definitely a heterosexual man's preferred means of ending sexual activity. Already by the 1950s, Kinsey had concluded that some men (often the more educated) are much more interested in eroticism and activities peripheral to intercourse than others. Kinsey also noted that this peripheral activity was not continuously applied to consistent anatomy. He concluded that when women masturbate, they stimulate themselves (the clitoris) up until orgasm as men do. He concluded that women are slower to respond with a lover because of the discontinuity of sexual stimulation that men supply.

In later decades, the greater awareness of the role of the clitoris in female orgasm, meant that the clitoral glans was added to the list of anatomy that men were told to stimulate to arouse a woman. Consequently, most women most of the time are assumed to orgasm from cunnilingus, manual stimulation of the clitoris or even the breasts. The variety of anatomy is never rationalised. The comparison with male orgasm techniques, which always focus on the penis, is never made. Most men focus on intercourse for their own sexual release, so if they offer foreplay (stimulation other than intercourse) at all, it is often to ensure that a woman's vagina is lubricated.[13]

2.3.3 Women depend on a lover to stimulate them to orgasm

Everyone applauds the idea that a man should care about his partner's orgasm.[14] But orgasm is an instinctive response to eroticism that occurs in our own brain not our partner's. When a couple's sex life falls apart, therapists focus on issues in the wider relationship rather than discuss sexual techniques. This is because sex is a male need and women need emotional factors to be amenable to offering regular intercourse. Shere Hite's research confirmed that women engage in sex for emotional reasons. Women rarely refer to eroticism or sexual pleasure at all. Intercourse for men equates to masturbation for responsive women. These activities provide the most rewarding and reliable way for a person to obtain a sexual release.

I have never been embarrassed about sex. I enjoyed erotic fiction from my teenage years and had high expectations for my sex life. Early in my relationship with my long-term partner, we decided to talk to marriage guidance counsellors. A man and a woman worked together. They recommended abstaining from intercourse to allow time to explore each other's bodies and find other ways of enjoying physical intimacy. The implication was that difficulties were due to timidity or inhibition. Yet, even though nothing worked, I had always been willing to explore sex play with a lover.

I had masturbated myself to orgasm since the age of 17. I was never asked for details. Given the widespread belief that female masturbation is common, it is surprising that no one asks a woman to explain her masturbation techniques. It is often suggested that a woman can masturbate herself to orgasm with a lover. No one ever challenges this suggestion. Many men want the satisfaction of believing that they have caused their lover's orgasm (especially through thrusting). I found that the two experiences of masturbation and sex with a lover had nothing in common, either in terms of psychological erotic arousal or the physical stimulation technique used.

The counsellors had no explanations for my experiences. Equally they provided no insights into how other women achieve orgasm with a lover. They didn't specify the anatomy or explain the turn-ons that might cause women to experience the kind of erotic arousal that makes orgasm possible. The man told us that he was aroused by the idea of a woman wearing a bra that exposes her nipples. The woman never referred to her turn-ons. Yet the inherent assumption was that women are aroused just as men are. At the end of the sessions there were no solutions or revelations. It seemed that I was expected to accept things as they were. I was meant to be aroused by the stimulation my partner provided and, if I wasn't, it was just bad luck.

III   Similarities between male and female responsiveness

The similarities between male and female responsiveness include:

- Mental arousal must always precede physical stimulation;
- The mind responds to erotic stimuli: concepts or objects;
- Orgasm is a one-off release followed by a recovery period;
- Orgasm involves identifying with the penetrating male;
- The same organ, the erectile phallus, is involved in orgasm;
- Orgasm is achieved by massaging the corpora cavernosa;
- Stimulation that leads to orgasm is applied instinctively;
- Stimulation and a focus on eroticism continue until orgasm;
- Orgasm comes at the end of activity intended to achieve it; and
- Orgasm is not the goal of sexual activity with a lover.

One area that has been lacking in all the research is a unification theory (if you like) for the human nervous response that is called orgasm. There is an assumption that orgasm means the same thing to men and women. Yet people believe they are achieved in completely different ways.[15] I have challenged this assumption because it makes no sense that the characteristics of sexual responsiveness would differ between the sexes or because of sexual orientation. I have concluded that orgasm must be a response common to all. My work attempts to define how orgasm is achieved by anyone.

I have compared my experience of arousal and orgasm with the equivalent responses that I have observed in my partners and in the sexual behaviours of men in everyday life. I have described the characteristics that male and female responsiveness have in common. I have also highlighted those areas where men and women respond differently to sexual stimuli. I present a definition of what is involved in sexual response. Essentially an erotic stimulus, a mental trigger, causes the brain to send blood to the genitals. This nervous excitement motivates us to stimulate our erectile organ.

I have found parallels between male responsiveness and my own. Before orgasm is possible, I always need to be mentally aroused (as a direct result of explicitly erotic stimuli). I feel no embarrassment in admitting this because my pleasure derives from the erotic aspects of my fantasies. I have never met another woman who understands the role of psychological erotic stimuli in achieving orgasm. I have concluded that women's reluctance to talk about orgasm is due to a lack of confidence in their experiences, which are unsensational compared to those portrayed in erotic fiction. I think this lack of confidence explains why women cannot provide explicit details.

3.1 Mental arousal must always precede physical stimulation

The only reason women are assumed to orgasm without ever being mentally aroused is because most women are unaware of what is involved in sexual response. They observe men and conclude that only physical stimulation is required to achieve orgasm. Women overlook the significance of a man having an erection. They are oblivious to (or thoroughly shocked by) what goes on inside the male brain. Women define orgasm in terms of the emotional feelings they experience rather than eroticism as men do. But orgasm must arise in the same way regardless of sex or orientation.

Even without any scientific understanding, we can draw conclusions about how men achieve orgasm by observing their orgasm techniques. A man massages the shaft of his penis to get an erection only once he is ready to engage in sexual activity, which means that his brain also responds. A psychological erotic trigger causes the brain to increase the blood flow to the genitals. Young boys may have erections spontaneously in non-erotic situations. Many younger men wake every morning with an erection. But for the most part, adult men are aroused because their minds respond to erotic stimuli, such as the physical or imagined presence of an attractive partner.

Kinsey found that some men do not fantasise when masturbating. We think of fantasy as a consciously imagined scenario that overrides or embellishes a person's current actual circumstances. But the critical issue is whether the brain is positively affected by erotic stimuli (either visual, imagined or sensory). No adult can orgasm while they are solving a problem or engaging in conversation. Adults orgasm as a result of the brain's response to eroticism, which motivates them to stimulate their genitals instinctively.[16]

A man assumes that arousal equates to physical stimulation because he discounts any preliminary mental activity. A man can be aroused by erotic stimuli throughout the day. So by the time he gets an opportunity for sexual activity (even masturbation), a man wants to apply physical stimulation to complete his arousal cycle. But there are no real-world triggers that cause female arousal. So a woman is not constantly aroused. Personally, I knew from masturbation, that orgasm involves taking a state of mental arousal to orgasm by applying instinctive stimulation. But I did not apply this knowledge to sex. Later I realised that I was not responding with a lover because I was not aroused. I concluded that I could not use surreal fantasy with a lover because of the level of concentration on fantasy required. My lover is not a sex object. I am not aroused by his nudity or his genitals. I am not even aroused by the idea of his erect penis penetrating my vagina.

3.1.1 The mind responds to erotic stimuli: concepts or objects

No boy reaches puberty and consciously decides to be aroused by girls. It just happens. If it doesn't, he may have a very low sex drive. If a boy is aroused by boys, he is probably homosexual. If a boy is aroused by both sexes, he may be bisexual. No one consciously chooses what concepts, body parts or objects cause their arousal. Mental arousal occurs subconsciously or not at all. This aspect of sexual response is poorly understood.

When I ask men to name female erotic turn-ons, they cannot. But they do not think that their ignorance is significant. They suggest that only a woman can explain her turn-ons. Yet women know (as everyone does) what turns men on. Women are not geniuses of deduction. Male turn-ons are obvious because men refer to them every day. We see movies where men talk about the female sexual anatomy that arouses them. We see men in movies surreptitiously trying to observe women bending over or undressing. We hear references to men (but never women) who are voyeurs.

Being attractive is advantageous for anyone. But female beauty has a special significance because of men's sexual appreciation of the female form. A man may view a woman as a sexual asset (trophy). Women do not objectify people as men do. So women are not aroused by real-world erotic triggers (such as anatomy) as men are. For example, men can urinate by the side of the road and women show no interest in observing a man's genitals. We assume that women respond with a lover just as men do. But men are usually mentally aroused well before they take their clothes off.[17]

Women have no idea how men experience erotic arousal. Women describe emotional and sensual feelings but refer to them as arousing or erotic. Women mistakenly assume that emotional stimuli (such as the sound of a lover's voice, kissing or caressing) cause arousal. But mental arousal depends on explicitly erotic stimuli (relating to genitals and penetration). Men are aroused by anatomy or by objects associated with sexual activity.

I noticed that I never fantasise about men I know in real life. The men in my fantasies are concepts, the idea of a man, or at least the imagined sexual thoughts in a man's head (as I assume them to be). I concluded that this form of fantasy, using conceptual men, effectively makes men into objects. A responsive woman can imagine herself being the receiver of intercourse and simultaneously imagine herself to be the penetrating male. I can be the person driving the activity and doing something sexual to another person. I focus on the act of entering a person's body with an aroused penis. Realising this, helped me see the possible parallels with the male experience.

17

3.1.2 Orgasm is a one-off release followed by a recovery period

With all the completely insane and goofy explanations, I get from women on the internet, it is tempting to believe that, somewhere, there must be women who are intelligent and sexually knowledgeable who could make a much better job of explaining their sexuality. I don't believe this is the case. Most women keep quiet because they know that they don't know. The ones who speak up are those who are unaware of their own ignorance.

Women get angry and defensive when asked to explain their beliefs about how they orgasm. They boast about orgasm by reflecting beliefs about female orgasm in the society around them. They do not expect to be held personally accountable for these fantasies. But I am challenging these orgasm claims by women (and on behalf of women) based on erotic fiction. By reporting women's orgasm claims, Alfred Kinsey promoted multiple orgasms. Yet even he concluded that these were only peaks of arousal.[18]

A woman knows how men achieve orgasm, not from sex education or because men tell her but, because she can observe her lovers. A woman sees a man take action to obtain the stimulation he needs for orgasm. Likewise, women are aware of male turn-ons because men talk about what turns them on in everyday life. Men do not learn these same things about women because women never refer to erotic turn-ons that cause their arousal. Similarly with a lover, women do not actively obtain the stimulation that they need for orgasm. Men cannot know more than women know themselves. Scientists research female orgasm because they hope to discover what the average couple has missed. But if women routinely had orgasms with a lover, everyone would be familiar with the turn-ons that cause female arousal and the physical stimulation that is required for female orgasm.

Any activity that has orgasm as its goal, ends when orgasm is achieved. This is logical for a number of reasons. The goal has been achieved. Our mental focus on eroticism has achieved its purpose. There is no further excitement from pursuing it. Once orgasm is achieved, blood flows away from the genitals. We feel pleasantly relaxed. We do not obtain pleasure (rather discomfort) by continuing the stimulation that caused orgasm. Anyone who can orgasm, understands how their own sexual arousal works, the erotic turn-ons and the specific stimulation technique involved because it is a reliable process. Arousal can be reliably achieved within our own personal level of responsiveness. Younger men can orgasm almost every time they have the opportunity. But older men, and women all their lives, have to wait until enough time has passed for sexual tension to accumulate.

3.1.3 Orgasm involves identifying with the penetrating male

Some women suggest that female arousal depends on emotional stimuli. I do not think I ever accepted this idea. But it is difficult to discount the experience of others. I slowly concluded that they are mistaken. This fact led me to a further conclusion that arousal is not a common place experience for women. Consequently, most women have no idea what it entails.

I wondered why I always have to focus so intensely on erotic fantasy before I was conscious of any arousal. I have concluded that I am never conscious of any state of arousal except as a precursor to masturbation. I also wondered why I needed complete privacy and silence to achieve the arousal I needed for orgasm. I have concluded that this is also due to the intensity of mental focus that is required to generate arousal from nothing. Women do not have the advantages men have of hormonal or biological arousal. Nor do they respond during the day to real-world erotic triggers.

Although Kinsey noted that women engage in sexual activity without having an orgasm, he did not relate this finding to female masturbation techniques. Most of Kinsey's data came from private interviews. He also observed individuals engaging in sexual activity, including a woman who masturbated by lying face down on the bed. Her instinctive rhythmic thrusting of her hips reminded Kinsey of the action of the penetrating male during intercourse.[19] I had never thought of how it might look to an observer before. When we act instinctively, we do not tend to wonder why we do so. Our motivation is subconscious and the activity feels natural.

Even when one accepts that the clitoris is the organ responsible for female orgasm, there is a further intellectual step in understanding women's responsiveness. The parallel in anatomy is only part of a bigger picture. Responsiveness is a characteristic of male reproductive function. Male orgasm triggers the reproductive process. Women are only capable of orgasm because they have anatomy and psychology that has evolved from the sexual development of the male. Hence the rarity of female orgasm.

Masturbation involves a woman stimulating anatomy equivalent to the penis (the phallus). Orgasm involves the erectile sex organ (penis or clitoris). So, by masturbating, a woman is instinctively (not consciously) emulating (both mentally and physically) the penetrating male. A woman focuses on the male role (as penetrator) in intercourse when she instinctively uses fantasy to view sexual activity from the perspective of the penetrating male. The pelvic muscular action involved, when a woman masturbates in this fashion, also emulates the copulatory movements of a man in intercourse.

19

3.2 The same organ, the erectile phallus, is involved in orgasm

The erectile organs (penis and clitoris) develop from the same anatomy in the foetus called the genital tubercle. The penis and clitoris have crura alongside the corpora cavernosa that cause tumescence.[20] It is inconceivable that the organ responsible for male orgasm would not be the same organ that is responsible for female orgasm. Some sexologists suggest that intercourse, which stimulates the vagina, can have a secondary effect on the clitoris because the two organs are adjacent to each other or because parts of these two organs are connected. This is like saying that men should stimulate the testes because they are adjacent and connected to the penis.

Kinsey noted that after adolescence, men need specific penile stimulation to achieve orgasm. Whether men engage in intercourse, masturbation or oral sex (fellatio), the penis is always involved. Equally, stimulation involves massaging the shaft of the penis that contains the corpora cavernosa. These structures trap blood and cause an erection. Being erect is what makes the penis so erotically sensitive (in a pleasurable way). The clitoris is an internal organ that is only ever tumescent (not rigid like the penis).

Confusingly when people refer to the clitoris, they usually mean the clitoral glans, which is the only externally visible part of the clitoral organ. Consequently many people assume that women should orgasm from stimulation of the glans. But if we look at the parallel for men, they do not typically achieve orgasm by stimulating the glans of the penis. Masturbation involves pulling the outer layer of skin up and down the shaft of the penis. This stimulation of the shaft by the hand provides more specific and effective stimulation than that provided by penetrative sex. The effectiveness of penetrative sex relies on the psychological turn-on for the penetrating male of thrusting his erect penis into another person's body orifice.

When I compare my masturbation technique to a man's, there are obvious parallels. I start by focusing on a fantasy to generate the arousal that I know from experience is vital to achieving orgasm. Without this mental response, stimulation is ineffective. The concept of penetrative sex as an erotic act (also of violation) is key to my ability to become aroused. Unlike a man, this mental process is conscious and never occurs spontaneously. I use the fingers of both hands to push down over the clitoral glans using a rhythmic technique (much slower than a man's). Once aroused, I press down further either side of the labia, where the internal clitoral organ (containing the corpora cavernosa) is located, near the entrance to the vagina. This stimulation technique is incompatible with sociable sexual activity.

3.2.1 Orgasm is achieved by massaging the corpora cavernosa

As part of my research, I came across references to the corpora cavernosa. These are cylindrical structures within the shaft of the penis that run down either side of the urethra (the central tube that urine and semen come down). It has also been established that the body (or shaft) of the internal clitoral organ has equivalent structures. The corpora cavernosa are mentioned in both Kinsey's work and Hite's. So they have been known about for some time. The corpora cavernosa trap blood and cause the penis to become erect. So it seems logical to assume that they are likely to have a similar role (even if largely defunct or less efficient) in the clitoral organ.[21]

Our instinctive sexual responses occur within the body or the brain. So it is difficult to provide hard evidence of the physiological processes involved. From observing my partners, men clearly start by getting an erection. The flaccid penis has little sensitivity. A man can enjoy having his flaccid penis stimulated gently by mouth. But the pleasure probably comes from the turn-on of having a partner interacting with his genitals. It is primarily once the penis is erect that men seem to enjoy the optimal pleasure of stimulation. Men always stimulate the penis directly in order to achieve orgasm. Intercourse, fellatio and male masturbation all stimulate the penis directly. The stimulation technique is consistent. It involves massaging the shaft of the penis (containing the corpora cavernosa) and over the glans.

When I masturbate, as I get close to orgasm, I push my fingers down into the spongey tissue either side of the labia majora. I also thrust forward with my hips and tense my buttock muscles from behind to create internal pressure. This stimulation technique didn't make sense to me. But it always had to be the same. Later I learned that the clitoral crura (connected to the corpora cavernosa) are located either side of the labia majora. I concluded that my stimulation technique massages (as much as one can) the body of internal clitoral organ. This would mean that there were parallels between my own and the male experience of arousal and orgasm. This theory is difficult to prove categorically but it is certainly a possible explanation.

I realised that female masturbation involves emulating the male role in intercourse. The clitoris is never erect but the clitoris can be tumescent. I could see and feel my physical arousal in middle age (unconnected with any mental arousal). When masturbating, I feel mild physical excitement that I interpret as my body responding to the fantasy I am thinking about. The male response to turn-ons is rapid. A responsive woman needs to generate arousal consciously, which takes time and depends on being alone.

3.2.2 Stimulation that leads to orgasm is applied instinctively

We all assume we already know everything there is to know about sex and sexuality. Even though we have never had a sex education (because no one has), we are confident that no other knowledge (beyond what we already know) exists. Certainly, there is a lack of factual information. But equally none of us ever reads the research that has been done. The findings have been rejected because they are non-sensational (compared with much more popular fantasies) or they are rejected for emotional or political reasons.

When I discovered orgasm, I did not act on information that I had been given. I did not approach masturbation by copying something I had seen in movies, something I had read in erotic fiction or been told about. I did not discover orgasm because I bought a vibrating gadget. I was not trying to have an orgasm. I was thinking about an erotic scenario and wiggling my hips instinctively. It felt reassuring to be lying face down. It was comforting to have my hands over my vulva. I had an orgasm from the instinctive stimulation I applied as a result of my mind's response to eroticism. The first time, orgasm occurred unexpected. Thereafter, I used the same approach over decades to enjoy orgasm reliably.[22] Nothing else worked.

I have always been sure about orgasm. There was no doubting that I experienced arousal and orgasm because I could achieve them both reliably each time. It was a predictable and repeatable experience. All I needed was the initial trigger of a vague response in my genitals on contemplating self-stimulation. Every time (without exception) I had to stimulate my clitoral organ in a highly specific way. Every time I had to achieve an intense (in a way that blocked out all other mental activity) focus on a highly explicit, often surreal (activity that I could not achieve in real life) fantasy scenario.

But I never linked this experience to intercourse. They were always two quite separate experiences from the start. The reason for them being separate was that masturbation was such a limited activity. It had nothing to do with the social environment of sexual pleasuring with a lover. Because I engaged in the activity instinctively, I had no idea why masturbation had such specific characteristics. I always had to masturbate in the same way.

I didn't understand why orgasm was such a limited experience. But I spent decades reading the research and thinking about my own experience. I spent time writing down exactly what I was doing to achieve orgasm. I considered the orgasm claims of other women. I searched the internet for information about anatomy and other aspects of sexuality that I am unfamiliar with (such as gay sex). I slowly formulated some possible theories.

22

3.2.3 Stimulation and a focus on eroticism continue until orgasm

Imagine you are a woman. Your partner asks you to masturbate him to orgasm. Each time you do this, you would notice that the length of time varies. The amount of stimulation required differs. This is because a man's initial state of arousal varies and his engagement in the activity (thoughts in his head) vary from occasion to occasion. Imagine if you said that when masturbating him, you will only offer this stimulation for a set period of time determined by you that has nothing to do with how long he needs the stimulation to last for. He wouldn't be very happy, would he? Stimulation must continue until orgasm is reached. Likewise, a woman cannot determine how long intercourse will last. Consequently, a woman cannot orgasm from intercourse regardless of the anatomy assumed to be involved.

Stimulation can be physical or psychological. We can be stimulated physically by doing something and we can be stimulated psychologically by thinking about the same thing. For example, we can compare our enjoyment of eating a meal with the enjoyment of thinking about eating a meal.

Men may think that arousal is the period of time when they obtain physical stimulation with a partner or through masturbation. But arousal occurs before we contemplate physical stimulation. This is because genital stimulation is only effective (likely to lead to orgasm) once we are mentally aroused (when men have an erection and responsive women use fantasy).

Women refer to fantasy as if it is optional. Some women say their fantasies involve emotional situations such as an affair, swinging or a loving relationship. But these are social situations for a woman. They are also based almost wholly on intercourse. My conclusion is that orgasm is an instinctive response that arises when our minds are focused on explicit eroticism.

There are graduations in arousal from stone cold to the instant before orgasm occurs. But in the early stages, we may be a long way off achieving orgasm (except younger men and boys). As adults we may need an appropriate situation or a relaxed mind and an opportunity for privacy before we can focus our minds on obtaining both the mental stimulus and the physical stimulation that we know (from experience) are a requirement of orgasm.[23]

In the context of achieving orgasm, erotic stimuli have to be more than a short skirt or a cleavage. In order to reach orgasm, a man needs to focus on an image or concept that relates to explicit penetrative sexual activity. I have found that my fantasies that I use to achieve orgasm also have to be extremely explicit and focus on conceptual aspects of penetrative sex.

3.3 Orgasm comes at the end of activity intended to achieve it

I used my own experience of sexual activity with a lover to draw conclusions about women's use of behaviours in responding to sexual scenarios in the way that men appreciate. Sociable sexual activity focuses on male orgasm because of men's acute arousal. Due to their lack of arousal, women may provide turn-ons and stimulation to assist with male orgasm. Intercourse is a mating act. So intercourse always ends with male orgasm[24] because it triggers ejaculation. In order to orgasm, we have to ensure that stimulation continues up until orgasm is reached. This is the easiest way to explain why intercourse cannot cause female orgasm, no matter what female sexual anatomy intercourse is supposed to inadvertently stimulate.

If women were able to orgasm with a lover, they would dictate the anatomy that they wanted to stimulate or to have stimulated by a lover. The anatomy would not vary from woman to woman or from occasion to occasion. The fact is that men stimulate the female anatomy that arouses them. Then it is assumed that women should orgasm from this stimulation even though it is directed towards different anatomy and never to the point of orgasm. It is simply assumed that women have an orgasm at some point before sexual activity ends (always co-incident with male orgasm and ejaculation).

It was decades later that I came to appreciate that my arousal worked very differently to male arousal. Male arousal is acute, intense, immediate, highly physical and easy to resolve as an orgasm. My own arousal was subconscious. I was rarely aware of being aroused at all. It was only when I was alone and able to focus on mental fantasy that I had any sense of arousal. Even then the feelings were muted. They were not intense or acute. They certainly did not easily cause spontaneous orgasm. It took extreme concentration and some perseverance on my part to achieve orgasm.

I realised that because of embarrassment no one ever talks about the specifics of sexual activity. I never really appreciated this until I attempted to do the same. Kinsey was a good start. But, as an empirical scientist, he recorded what the general population told him. He did not feel obliged to provide explanations where these were not apparent. Specifically, he did not explain how arousal and orgasm are achieved. It has taken me decades to consider the possibilities and even to record my own experiences. We lack practice in talking about our sexual responses and intimate experiences. We don't have any structure to build on because we have no source of accumulated knowledge. It's like being in the Stone Age, before the wheel was invented, and trying to explain how a combustion engine works.

3.3.1 Orgasm is not the goal of sexual activity with a lover

Orgasm has become a key word in talking about sex. Certainly, the most important aspect of women's participation in sex is whether they have an orgasm. Naturally, male orgasm is not an issue because it occurs reliably.

My partner explained to me that orgasm was not his key focus during sex. Sexual release was a given but he wanted to extend the pleasure of thrusting and his own arousal. At first, I found this difficult to accept. There is so much talk of orgasm. It seems that sex and orgasm are one and the same thing. Certainly, men's view seems to be: what is the point of sexual activity without orgasm? That is how they seem to evaluate women's experiences. It explains the pressure that men put on women to say they orgasm every time they engage in sexual activity with a lover.[25] So why do men apply different expectations for women than they do for themselves?

I think the answer is that men see female orgasm as a token of approval. It reassures a man that he has delivered the pleasure he assumes a woman experiences from sexual activity. Female orgasm, in some way, allows a man to equate the female experience to his own. This means he can feel less guilty about sex being primarily a male pleasure, which in truth, it is.

But equally, as a woman and an observer of male sexuality, it always seemed to me that a man is obliged to continue sexual activity until he ejaculates (co-incident with male orgasm). Very rarely does a man give up on orgasm and accept that he will end sexual activity with a lover without achieving orgasm. So the need for sexual release (orgasm and ejaculation) through thrusting seems to be important to men. The vital issue to understand is that men enjoy their arousal and the activity of thrusting for itself.

Orgasm ends a man's ability to engage in sexual activity of any kind because he loses his erection. But this is a characteristic of orgasm for anyone, even a woman, because orgasm ends activity focused on achieving it.

Orgasm occurs spontaneously and sporadically. That is to say, that we cannot predict the exact timing of our orgasm. It occurs as a result of the mental arousal reaching a climax in our head in combination with the physical stimulation, we apply to bring that mental arousal to a climax. We cannot orgasm on demand or exactly at the same time as our lover has their orgasm (which if a true orgasm, also occurs randomly). The timing of orgasm cannot be controlled consciously. It is only a faked orgasm that can be timed to occur at just the right moment to facilitate a lover's orgasm. The objective of a faked orgasm is to provide a turn-on for a male lover.

3.3.2 Male and female sexuality both contribute to reproduction

When I started researching my sexuality, I knew how to masturbate to orgasm so I wanted to know how women achieved the orgasms with a lover that I had never found possible. I was fortunate because my partner was a practical person and eager to explore my body and responses. It's just none of this exploration had ever unearthed any sensation that compared with masturbation where I used fantasy. I assumed other couples (regardless of whether the woman masturbates or not) would have had similar experiences and would be willing to share techniques for pleasuring a woman.

In fact, the silence has been universal. And it is not just women who are silent about their sexuality. Very few men ever comment in depth on explicit sexual issues and none have been able to comment with the collaboration of their female partner. Men seem to assume that a woman's sexuality involves her responding pleasurably to stimulation that men initiate.

I have struggled to understand the cover-up by women. I accept that some women have political motives but it didn't make sense that so many women would lie about sexual response. I have concluded that responsiveness is a unique experience unlike any other. So if you never have an orgasm, you can't possibly know what it feels like. For anyone who experiences orgasm, it is difficult to appreciate the extreme pressure women must be under to provide evidence of a responsiveness their lovers and the society around them assumes they should have.[26] Some women know that orgasm does not occur but others seem to imagine that it does somehow.

I have concluded that there is no reason why women should ever be responsive. Their minds and bodies are not intended to respond erotically. Sociable activity focuses on male orgasm, the reproductive priority. Male orgasm is essential to reproduction because it triggers the ejaculation of semen (containing spermatozoa). Intercourse is an act of impregnation that is necessary for a new life to be created. For this to happen, a woman must be amenable to allowing a man to thrust into her vagina until he ejaculates.

Men wouldn't like it if women refused to have sex because they were not aroused (as men do). Nor would men like it if women only engaged in intercourse to obtain their own orgasm. If intercourse truly stimulated a woman to orgasm, she might want intercourse to end before a man ejaculated. This is counter to the goal of reproduction. So reproduction relies on women's lack of responsiveness as much as male responsiveness. Given that the function of intercourse is to facilitate male orgasm, the misconception that intercourse causes female orgasm puts unfair pressure on men.

26

3.3.3 Both sexes enjoy emotional rewards from sexual intimacy

Whenever a man and a woman share physical intimacy, the man's arousal is very evident. A man's erection gives visual evidence, not only that he is aroused, but that he wants to obtain penile stimulation. He demonstrates this by massaging his erection. He is very appreciative when a partner offers to stimulate his penis by hand. He is even more overjoyed if a partner offers to stimulate his penis by mouth because fellatio is much more like the stimulation of intercourse than masturbation. Fellatio offers a similar warm and wet environment that a man enjoys when he penetrates a vagina.

A man may make love to a partner because of his joy over having an amenable lover who he assumes is willing to offer him an opportunity for intercourse. He admires his lover's body that causes his arousal and ultimately provides his sexual release. He may be aroused by every aspect of his lover's nudity because of the associations that he has with past or imagined activity that cause him to anticipate the pleasure of penetrative sex.

A woman does not provide such obvious visual evidence of her presumed arousal. Nor does her behaviour reflect her possible arousal in the way that a man's behaviour does. She does not indicate the anatomy that she would like to have stimulated by a partner nor does she massage her internal tumescence that she may be assumed to be experiencing. Moreover, she does not respond with the same kind of appreciation that a man shows when her lover stimulates every body part in an attempt to provoke a response. So eventually, any man tires of providing random stimulation and focuses on stimulating the anatomy that interests him. This is, of course, Nature's intent. Intercourse dominates our sex lives because it provides men's most rewarding sexual release and it is fairly effortless for a woman to provide.

Women focus on the upper body action of intercourse. They are oblivious to the genital action because intercourse provides no physical sensation and no erotic arousal. So women are sexually passive. A woman allows a man to explore and stimulate her body as he decides. Women never give directions and only rarely do they provide any feedback. Women refer to lovemaking because they interpret intercourse as a sign of male devotion. Women feel loved and reassured by this male need. For women, sexual activity with a lover is purely sensual. For a man, the opportunity for penetration means that touching equates to sexual arousal. This is because men associate intimacy with sexual opportunities. This causes confusion if we equate the male and female experiences of sex and intimacy with a lover.[27]

27

IV   Differences between male and female responsiveness

The differences between male and female responsiveness include:

- Orgasm is a vital aspect of male reproduction function;
- Men obtain an optimal sexual release from penetrative sex;
- Only men are aroused in anticipation of sexual activity;
- Only men are aroused by observing a partner's genitals;
- Women are sexually passive due to lack of erotic arousal;
- The penis is an external organ but the clitoris is internal;
- Male arousal is acute but female arousal is subconscious;
- Responsive women use surreal fantasy to generate arousal.
- For women, sexual attraction does not include erotic arousal; and
- Women offer sex as an emotional bonding mechanism.

My journey of reconciling my lack of responsiveness with portrayals of women's arousal in erotic fiction began the very first time I had sex. I was bitterly disappointed. I felt nothing physically from vaginal penetration. In the early weeks of my first relationship, I offered pleasuring and cooperated with intercourse in ways that I knew from erotic fiction were pleasing to men. I let my partner try to arouse me by stimulating all the obvious anatomy. Nothing got anywhere close to the response I experienced when masturbating alone by focusing on fantasies.[28] There was never any erotic arousal with a lover. But I never put this experience into words until much later when, during my research, I thought about this issue in more depth.

It was clear from the beginning that my lack of responsiveness was not a show-stopper. It did not deter my partner from wanting to continue engaging in sexual activity. Naturally, he tried all the stimulation techniques that are recommended. But nothing worked. There did not appear to be anything that could be done. My partner had a drive to engage in intercourse regardless of my response to it. I later concluded that intimate relationships essentially oblige women to offer men the opportunity for sexual release through intercourse because of men's regular arousal. Equally, society assumes that women are compensated for providing regular intercourse because of their desire for family and their consequent dependence on men.

My work presents my experience of masturbation and sexual activity with a lover. I explain the erotic stimuli that arouse me mentally. I describe the specific physical stimulation I use to orgasm. I present my conclusions for why these techniques are ineffective with a lover. I describe in detail the stimulation techniques that I have found to be pleasurable with a lover.

4.1 Orgasm is a vital aspect of male reproductive function

When I had intercourse for the first time (as a virgin) I was shocked that I felt no internal physical sensation of any kind. I was unaware that my lover had inserted his penis into my vagina. I could feel absolutely nothing from his penis thrusting into my body. The only reason I knew he had finished was because he withdrew his penis to avoid ejaculating into my vagina. I was worried that he had not used a condom but I was also shocked that I felt absolutely no sense of arousal. There was nothing about the whole scenario from start to finish that excited my mind. It was purely functional.

I was shocked by the lack of arousal and physical stimulation of intercourse. The stimulation part I could not have known about before because I was never motivated to stimulate the inside of my vagina. But there is a clue here. If the vagina was an erectile organ (in a way that made a woman conscious of her physical arousal) then a woman would be motivated to stimulate it herself. I could also have deduced the lack of erotic arousal beforehand. Boys know well before they have the opportunity for intercourse that they will be aroused by it. This is because they are aroused by the prospect of penetration (that they simulate by masturbating) as well as by the anatomy and the physical presence of an attractive potential partner.

When I have told others of my experience, no one expresses surprise. Nor do they offer any possible explanations. I assume they are amazed by my honesty. I'm not the first woman to complain about lack of orgasm with a lover. But I can explain how I achieve my own erotic arousal and orgasm. In order to experience arousal, a person must first be responsive. This is straightforward for men because their responsiveness is biological or hormonal. It occurs as an automatic part of adolescence and, importantly, in sociable, real-world situations (much to their embarrassment at times!). As a virgin, I was amazed by the physical evidence of my lover's erection and the ease with which he could be stimulated to orgasm. I had no comparable experience. For me, masturbation was a very private, solitary experience.

Men are proactive lovers due to their arousal and some men enjoy stimulating a woman's nude body before seeking intercourse. But regardless of whether a man is willing to spend time on foreplay to extend his own arousal, every man's ultimate goal is intercourse. This is because reproduction depends as much on male sex drive as it does on male orgasm. There is no point to a man having an orgasm if he is not motivated to have it with his penis inside a woman's vagina. Yet many women clearly have no conception of the sex drive that compels men to seek intercourse.[29]

4.1.1 Men obtain an optimal sexual release from penetrative sex

Sex drive has been defined in terms of the proactive role that men have in obtaining intercourse. Male sex drive is apparent from the way men behave. Men often view penetrative sex as a conquest. They know they have obtained something (intercourse) that women do not always want to give. Women, who seduce men, offer intercourse to get financial or emotional rewards. Men respond to physical affection by becoming aroused and consequently wanting penetrative sex. Kinsey disliked the term sex drive.

The issue is that sex drive depends on various factors. Firstly to engage in intercourse, a man needs an erection, which depends on erotic stimuli. Secondly, some men use masturbation more than others. Consequently, the men with the highest intercourse frequencies tend to be those who are less particular about their partners or the circumstances of sexual activity. Kinsey used orgasm frequency (related to general metabolic rate) as a measure of responsiveness. Nevertheless, I have noticed that once a man has a naked woman in front of him, he tends to have a strong desire for intercourse.

We talk about orgasm as if it is the be all and end all of sex. But if this were the case, we wouldn't need to have sex. We could all just masturbate instead. Sex drive is the biological urge a man experiences to thrust into a body orifice (vagina, mouth or rectum) with an erect penis until he ejaculates. Sex drive is instinctive and biological. It is not easily subdued by persuasion, by the risk of pregnancy or by a lack of reliable contraception.

When women refer to a sex drive, I have concluded that they don't understand the nature of the male phenomenon. Sex drive arises in the mind of an aroused male who is strongly motivated to obtain penetrative sex. Women are sexually passive with a lover. A woman cannot orgasm as the receiver of intercourse because she cannot control how long the stimulation will last for. So what is the purpose of female sex drive if it is not to achieve orgasm? By engaging in intercourse, a woman risks pregnancy. Why would a woman have a drive to be impregnated? A biological sex drive occurs automatically. It operates regardless of our conscious desires.

Women often say that they prefer sex to masturbation. This is because very few women are responsive enough to discover orgasm.[30] Lovemaking causes women to feel loved, admired and needed. A woman is reassured by male admiration. An emotional attachment is formed when a man demonstrates (not just says) that he cares about her. This male behaviour (that operates during an initial romance) seduces a woman into hoping that the relationship will provide the affectionate companionship she hopes for.

4.1.2 Only men are aroused in anticipation of sexual activity

Off the coast of France, at Cannes, there is an island where people are permitted to bathe nude. Nude bathing is popular in France, particularly along the south coast and there are many nudist beaches. My partner and I went there (not for that reason!) and walked around the island by the coast path. Knowing that I fantasise about homosexual erotica, my partner suggested that I might want to watch a couple of guys he spotted having sex on one of the secluded beaches. I was embarrassed and mortified. The idea of watching them horrified me. I felt that it would be wrong to intrude on their privacy. But what is difficult for a man to understand, is that my turn-ons are conceptual and not related to the reality of sexual action at all.

The reality of sexual activity for me is just what it is. The facts. There is no particular eroticism to it. Sure, it is portraying sexual activity. But it is too close to the reality, which is not arousing at all. Looking at genitals for me is just the same as looking at feet (and I don't have a foot fetish!). Sexual activity is similar but it focuses on two (or more) people's genitals interacting with each other. So what? This is just like people playing footsie under the table. It can be arousing for a man because he interprets this female behaviour as a sexual invitation. But for a woman footsie under the table is just a teasing game to arouse a man. It is not at all arousing.[31]

I enjoy reading about anal intercourse and fellatio but seeing two gay men in reality would not be remotely arousing for me. It would be excruciatingly embarrassing. My enjoyment of these activities comes from thinking about the mind of the penetrator and the idea of doing something to another person. My fantasies do not focus on close-up images of genitals. I can also masturbate while reading a book. When we read, we do not imagine focused images. We view the scene in fuzzy images. We concentrate on the feelings and thoughts of the participants. We see the scene from the perspective of one of the participants, particularly the penetrating male. We imagine how the receiver responds to a man's desire for penetration.

In my fantasies, the receiver is reluctant (in an accepting rather than a rejecting way). The penetrator is persuading the receiver to allow him to push his engorged penis into an orifice. My arousal comes from the idea that the receiver accepts fairly willingly an action that is done to them. This is different to the usual definition of rape. The scene is not violent or hateful. It is one that focuses on the penetrator's satisfaction in obtaining penetration regardless of the receiver's desire for it. This can be a disturbing concept for a woman who is always the receiver of intercourse in reality.

4.1.3 Only men are aroused by observing a partner's genitals

My partner likes to take photographs of my genitalia while we are having sex. Note that I have no similar desire to photograph his penis! He enjoys seeing my labia slightly swollen and the lubrication that comes from my vagina. One morning when I was busy eating breakfast, he walked up and put his phone in front of my face. It showed a closeup of my labia surrounded by pubic hair. He pointed out the glistening of the lubrication. I abruptly repulsed him saying that I did not want to see it. Despite his obvious joy and desire to share the image, I was irritated that he could be so oblivious to my dislike of genital images. I am not even conscious of any arousal with a lover. I might enjoy images of a little furry puppy but not images of my own genitals that are non-emotive folds of pink hairy flesh.

A man must find this hard to accept because images of genitals and reminders of sexual activity are so erotic for them.[32] Men don't appreciate that a woman cannot see her genitalia easily no matter what sexual activity she is engaged in. During masturbation alone, I lie face down and typically I have my eyes closed. Often it is night-time and the room is dark. I don't give any thought to my genitals and how they might look. My whole focus is on the fantasy in my head. The stimuli I respond to are not graphic or well-focused visual images. They are concepts that relate to penetration.

Naturally, the vagina is amazingly erotic to a heterosexual man given his drive to impregnate women. But I have never found the vagina remoting interesting. My only interaction with my vagina is when I push a tampon into it to absorb the blood flow during my period. So I fantasize about anal sex and fellatio both of which are much more taboo. I cannot feel anything from intercourse because the vagina expands easily to allow the penis to penetrate. Given many women's dislike of explicit genital details, I have concluded that women accept intercourse because there is no sensation. Both fellatio and anal sex represent activities that are much more explicit for a woman than vaginal intercourse. For this reason I have found homosexual erotic literature to be much more interesting and useful for arousal than heterosexual literature, which focuses on women's sexual anatomy.

But equally the attitude of the participants is different. In heterosexual erotica, the woman is often portrayed as a slut. She feels that what she is doing is whorish or obscene. Her thoughts focus on what the man is doing to her. Gay men are much more positive about the sexual pleasure they enjoy. They describe their lover's anatomy and responses in explicit detail. My fantasies are based on imaginary experiences rather than real ones.

4.2 Women are sexually passive due to lack of erotic arousal

Sexual reproduction even in plants (pollination) involves pollen being transferred (by wind or bees, for example) from the male reproductive part (the anther, part of the stamen) to the female reproductive part (the stigma, the tip of the pistil) of the plant. The male part is active and the female part is static. This is how sexual reproduction is defined throughout Nature.

In humans (and other mammals) the male is attracted to a female and is the initiator and the proactive driver of the mating act, by which a sperm cell (ejaculated from the penis) joins with an egg cell produced each month by the woman's body. The problem comes when we assume that an act of impregnation causes female orgasm. Male arousal is vital to reproduction because a man needs an erection to ejaculate into a vagina. Female responsiveness has no role in reproduction and nothing to do with intercourse.

The role of intercourse is well understood and the temptation is to believe that the mating act not only impregnates women but also provides them with an orgasm. In fact, the opposite is true. Intercourse is a risk-free activity for men but, for women, intercourse can cause pregnancy. Men think nothing of this risk because they are not the ones left holding the baby. This penalty means women instinctively avoid intercourse. Only masturbation alone allows a woman to enjoy risk-free sexual pleasure in the way that a man enjoys intercourse. We can say that women are sexually passive with a lover. But it is equally true to say that, due to her lack of arousal, a woman has a conscious choice over the man she allows to impregnate her.

Girls learn that men seek sexual contact (indeed all forms of physical intimacy). Women do not talk of their own desire to explore a man's body or need for penetration. They rarely refer explicitly to male sexual anatomy. They do not talk of sexual pleasure. They talk of their hopes for a considerate and charming lover who is respectful and caring. Women are concerned with the emotional responses that cause them to be amenable to allowing a man to obtain the sexual release that penetrating her body can provide. A woman interprets a man's admiration and devotion as romance.

I came to realise that a woman leaves the initiative to a man because she has no agenda of her own. Women refer to sexual arousal with a lover but these are emotional feelings.[33] They do not result from a mental focus on eroticism. A woman has many diffuse feelings in anticipation of intercourse but these sensations come from the mind and body preparing to accept an act of penetration, which is the most intimate act we can ever engage in. This is why women cannot explain erotic turn-ons with a lover.

4.2.1 The penis is an external organ but the clitoris is internal

The clitoris is the equivalent organ to the penis. They both develop from the genital tubercle in the foetus. The suggestion is that the two organs respond identically in the same scenarios (masturbation, intercourse and oral sex). Yet the penis is always stimulated directly. The clitoral organ is supposedly prodded through the walls of the vagina during intercourse or the glans is pulled by the thrusting penis. Equally, cunnilingus involves oral stimulation of the glans. How easily would a man orgasm, if his penis could only be stimulated in the same ways? No one seems to notice these very significant differences in the kinds of stimulation that are possible.

Imagine taking an erect penis and putting it inside a woman's body. First, the muscles that maintain an erection disappear. The clitoris has no equivalent muscles. It is only ever tumescent (never rigid). Second, you put this slightly swollen penis inside a woman's body so that only the glans (which is tiny) is visible externally. Then, as a man, you offer foreplay by sucking on the tiny glans before you offer to thump your penis against the sides of the vagina in the hope of stimulating the clitoral organ through the walls of the vagina while simultaneously pulling the glans as you thrust. Do men really think that this anatomical arrangement would equate to their own?

The penis is an external organ. It has muscles that trap the blood to create an erection, which is what makes the penis so sensitive. The clitoris is an internal organ, that is only ever tumescent (not erect like the penis). Researchers and educators appear to be unaware of the significance of these key differences.[34] Most women have no awareness of their clitoris or any tumescence. In middle age, I have been able to observe my own physical arousal by feeling the firmness either side of my labia majora. But there is no accompanying mental arousal or sense of sexual pleasure involved.

Some sex educators continue to promote the clitoris. But surely, if the clitoris gave women so much pleasure, they would not need to be told about it? Research indicates that women achieve orgasm most reliably alone. Many of these women also claim to orgasm with a lover. But women cannot orgasm from intercourse because stimulation does not continue to orgasm. Equally, if women could orgasm through (oral or manual) stimulation of the clitoral glans with a lover, they would have no reason to engage in intercourse. This calls into question the orgasms women claim to have from masturbation. If women could masturbate to orgasm, they would know that orgasm does not occur with a lover. If women's masturbation techniques worked with a lover, men would know how women orgasm too.

4.2.2 Male arousal is acute but female arousal is subconscious

When we look at how men orgasm, it is clear that a man must have an erection before he can attempt orgasm. Only when a man has an erection, does the penis respond (when the shaft is massaged) in such a way as to cause orgasm. This is true regardless of the activity a man engages in. So although an erection is a prerequisite for intercourse, a man also needs an erection before he can orgasm through masturbation or fellatio. A man becomes erect fairly quickly if he anticipates the prospect of sexual activity. This is such a well-established and accepted fact that we take it for granted.

Men experience acute arousal, both physical and mental. The penis becomes rigid, which is what makes stimulation highly pleasurable. Men's minds are also completely absorbed in the erotic stimuli of the scenario they anticipate (an opportunity to penetrate a lover with their erect penis). Men are intent on obtaining sexual release through thrusting to ejaculation.

Nevertheless, this male experience has not been applied to women. No one insists that women must be mentally aroused before they can orgasm. Most people are confused if you ask them to name female erotic turn-ons. They have no idea what you might be referring to. A woman's role in intercourse involves offering an orifice regardless of her own state of erotic arousal.

Female arousal with a lover is defined quite differently, even in pornography. Women display their bodies for male admiration. They wait for a lover to stimulate them. They provide come-ons and male turn-ons. Women's passivity and conscious behaviours clearly indicate that they are not experiencing sensational erotic arousal or physical pleasure. For older women, vaginal secretions may increase but there is no pleasure in this. Even when masturbating, female arousal is not as intense as male arousal. But a responsive woman can differentiate between the diffuse sensations with a lover and the focused arousal that arises from fantasy when alone.

It must seem ridiculous to a man that a woman is unsure about arousal.[35] Even for a responsive woman, her arousal is never, at any stage, the acute, physically obvious and highly conscious experience that men have. Even when masturbating, female arousal is felt as a semi-subconscious feeling of mild excitement. A responsive woman feels a barely discernible, slight tingling sensation that she learns to associate with arousal. When she has sex for the first time, a woman notices the contrast with masturbation alone but she does not appreciate that her inability to orgasm is due to her lack of mental arousal. This is because her arousal, even when alone, although critical to the activity, is a relatively insignificant physical phenomenon.

4.2.3 Responsive women use surreal fantasy to generate arousal

Before I started my research, I hadn't appreciated that my experience was so unusual. Reading Hite's work in my early twenties, reassured me that I was not alone. Both Kinsey and Hite documented many women who knew that orgasm is rarely possible with a lover. But in many years of talking about sex on the internet, not one woman has come forward to confirm my experience. It must be difficult for others to understand what this feels like. If it was not for Shere Hite, I would assume that I am on the wrong planet.

I assumed initially that other women were talking about the same experience with a lover. Later I realised that women do not understand the need for mental arousal. They think that by responding to male lovemaking, they have orgasms based on emotional feelings.[36] Men always stimulate the penis to orgasm and they need erotic turn-ons (usually visual and supplied by a lover). Women also need consistent stimulation from beginning to end of sexual activity. But more importantly they need to be aroused in their minds. Yet no one can name any female erotic turn-ons with a lover.

I have spent a long time thinking about how I achieve arousal and orgasm. This was more difficult than it sounds. When I masturbate, I use fantasy to block out the real world and to transport myself into a scenario where I can become conscious of my own erotic arousal. The individuals in my fantasies are not based on real people. I focus on the penis and the urge to penetrate. I instinctively put myself psychologically in the role of the penetrating male. I have concluded that this is because the anatomy, the clitoris, is equivalent to the male anatomy. I need to be alone because of the intense mental focus on erotic fantasy that I need in order to generate my arousal.

Lying face down is fundamental to making orgasm possible. The hands rest naturally in the right position over the vulva. I can rock my hips rhythmically from side to side. I can clench my buttock muscles when arousal starts to build. It is an ultimate comfort position, in which I feel safe and secure. I also close my eyes (except when I am reading erotic passages). I have concluded that this is due to the intense nature of the mental focus I need in order to be able to tap into my subconscious physical arousal.

Kinsey found that women take an average of 4 minutes to masturbate to orgasm. It depends where you count from. The difficulty is that it can take a while to get the necessary focus on a fantasy for arousal to kick in. Orgasm can take a minute or two. But often it takes longer because of the fantasy element. But 4 minutes is a good estimate of something that is difficult to estimate accurately, even on the basis of one woman's experience.

4.3 For women, sexual attraction does not include erotic arousal

Women are attractive to men because their bodies cause intense male arousal. Women are attracted to other women because female bodies are more sensual and less overtly sexual than male bodies. Men are attractive to other men because of their easy arousal. Heterosexual women respond to men's desire for penetrative sex to please their lover and to cement a supportive, loving relationship that they hope will last over the long-term.

I have always liked men. Foremost I am attracted by a person's mind. I like a man who has a sense of fun and who makes an interesting companion. But when I am attracted to a man, I do not respond erotically. For me, sexual attraction relies on forming an emotional attachment. Women want a lover who demonstrates affection. They want to be touched, caressed or hugged. They enjoy spending companionable time with a lover who demonstrates caring behaviours. Men want sexual love based on achieving a sexual release. Women feel nurturing, platonic love. A woman is motivated to care for her lover as she does her children. It is not a sexual love.

Naturally, I enjoy it when a man is attracted to me. When a man is aroused by a woman, he pays her special attention. He singles her out and enjoys her company. He listens or appears to. He maintains eye contact and smiles approvingly at what she says. He is attentive to her feelings and tries to please her. It is very gratifying. A woman can have strong emotional responses to male devotion. Some women assume this response equates to arousal. But it does not assist with orgasm. It is the female body preparing for intercourse (blood flows to the genitals and the vagina is lubricated).

I am not attracted to women. Their behaviour of displaying their body for admiration does not impress me. This display of anatomy works well for men but, even if a man were to display himself, it would do nothing for me. Men like sexual anatomy and provocative behaviours aimed at arousing them. So some women promote their bodies but they have no interest in discussing their sexuality, enjoyment of eroticism or sexual pleasuring.

I have concluded that before offering regular sex to a long-term partner, most women need to have formed an emotional attachment. Men are always physically and mentally aroused with a lover but women are not. This is why women naturally focus on upper body lovemaking, kissing and caressing.[37] Men focus on lower body genital stimulation because of their arousal. So men and women approach their relationships very differently regardless of orientation. Lesbians have long-term, often platonic, loving relationships. Gay men are much more likely to be highly promiscuous.

4.3.1 Women offer sex as an emotional bonding mechanism

A woman may believe that she has orgasms with her lover. But if she is unwilling to have the same experience with an attractive stranger, it is the relationship rather than the act itself that is giving her pleasure. Her pleasure derives from the emotional significance of the act within the relationship she has with her lover. This explains why women are much less promiscuous than men on average. Of course, there are women who will have sex with any man they come across. They are undiscerning about their sexual partner. But this is true for many fewer women than it is for men.

Just as there are women who use the words arousal, orgasm and erotic without appreciating what these words mean to men, there are men who use the word love without having any idea what it means to a woman. Some women describe their experiences in terms of arousal in order to meet male expectations for their sexuality. Equally, some men describe their experiences in terms of romantic love because the concept is more acceptable to women than crude sexual urges. It may be that men experience a little of the emotional sensations that women feel, just as women experience a little of the arousal that men feel. But male arousal can be overwhelming. Likewise women can feel a strong emotional connection.[38]

A man's response to a woman's body, causes him to feel an emotional connection with her based on his own arousal. When a woman responds positively by allowing a man to obtain his sexual release from penetrating her body, she completes the emotional bonding process. Men would never do this. Not just because they need to obtain their own sexual release but because they would never waste their time on non-arousing sexual activity.

People are quick to blame a woman or her lover for ignorance or poor technique, if female orgasm does not occur. But I have paid money to a sex clinic only to be told that I am very normal. No one had any solutions. But more importantly, they had no explanations. No one could confirm either the anatomy or the erotic turn-ons involved in these orgasms women are assumed to have routinely with a lover. These orgasms may be common in erotic fiction but the sensationalism indicates their rarity in reality.

Women seem to think that basic facts, such as the anatomy and turn-ons involved in orgasm, are somehow personal to them. These facts should be common knowledge. Women think that being asked to be explicit about orgasm is an infringement of their privacy rights. But orgasm with a lover is supposed to be a common experience. Every woman in the population, millions of women, are believed to achieve orgasm with a lover every time.

4.3.2 Some men want a lover to provide a response to intercourse

The basic male sexual function is instinctive. It is satisfied relatively easily by intercourse. Kinsey concluded that the vast majority of men (including the less educated) use intercourse as a quick (biological and functional) means of sexual release. They do not look for a response (erotic or emotional) from a lover. They do not need reassurance. Neither do they look for erotic turn-ons. So for women (probably the majority) who have a male partner who needs no erotic feedback, intercourse only lasts for an average of 2 minutes. This is hardly onerous and explains why so few women complain about the overhead of providing a man with a regular sexual outlet.

By thinking about how other mammals mate, I came to appreciate that intercourse is effectively a male assault. I also came across a reference to bull queers. These are heterosexual men who rape other men in male prisons. It seems that they like a victim who puts up a fight (called wigglers). I thought about this and it occurred to me that the resistance scenario is a natural turn-on. It explains why many fantasies (of both sexes) include rape or BDSM. The penetrating male obtains gratification from the victim's vocal objections and attempts to resist being penetrated by his penis.

I knew from my own experience that consensual intercourse provides little stimulation for a woman. Both the psychological turn-on and the physical stimulation of intercourse are enjoyed by the penetrating male. But it occurred to me that if we accept that intercourse has evolved from a mating act, which is effectively an act of male assault, then it's possible that men have also evolved a desire for a partner's response. This need is not based on an erotic response as such but can be satisfied by any noise and body movements that emulate a resisting partner. A man interprets this behaviour as a turn-on. Men assume that a woman can feel the penis thrusting into her vagina. But the rape victim objects to an act that is imposed on them with violence or hatred. This theory also explains the erotic feedback that porn actresses provide and the pressure on women to fake orgasm.[39]

I learned early on (as well as from erotic fiction) that a man appreciates some erotic feedback. A man enjoys a lover who moves with his rhythm, caresses and kisses him. A woman can move her hips to assist with penile stimulation. Kinsey highlighted that only a minority of men are concerned with a lover's response. Only some men (often the more educated) are interested in peripheral erotic concepts and activities other than intercourse. Kinsey suggested that more sensitive and imaginative men look for feedback from a lover. But this makes sex much more onerous for a woman.

4.3.3 Women may use behaviours to provide turn-ons for a lover

My first boyfriend was more than 6 years older than me. I was a virgin and he had plenty of sexual experience from one-night stands and also from longer-term relationships with women. It was natural that the first time we had intercourse, he was proactive in leading the activity. I just waited for something to happen. Nothing did. I was amazed and devastated that the whole experience was totally lacking in both physical and erotic sensation.

Thereafter I was quick to show initiative and explore my lover's body and his responsiveness. I thought that the penis was an amazing phenomenon. I certainly had nothing to compete with the attention-grabbing changes that occur when a man is sexually aroused. I was fascinated by the way in which his penis grew in my hand and then shrivelled back to its tiny size after he had ejaculated. I enjoyed kissing him and touching him because of his easy response and evident pleasure from the physical interaction. I accepted his desire to stimulate me in a similar way. But none of it worked the miracles for me that it did for him. My body seemed to be inert to all forms of stimulation, whether directly genital or general body stimulation.

Rather than switching off and losing interest in activity that did nothing for me, I decided to take a more proactive role that focused on pleasuring my partner. I felt that by doing this, I was demonstrating my lack of sexual inhibition and my enjoyment of activity focused on my lover's arousal and orgasm. I had read a great deal of erotic literature and was familiar with the techniques for pleasuring a man. Years later, I appreciated that male orgasm is the goal of sociable sexual activity. A woman orgasms alone.

Although I assumed a proactive role, this role focused on pleasuring my lover. I had nothing to offer in terms of what he could do to pleasure me. I was open to him trying whatever he could think of. But cunnilingus did nothing for me. Manual stimulation of the clitoral glans was uncomfortable. The techniques that I used alone were not compatible with sexual activity with a lover. Not only was it impossible to achieve the mental block-out that I needed to focus on surreal fantasy but the position[40] I needed to assume was incompatible with penetrative sex or interaction with a lover.

Responsiveness occurs subconsciously. We have no conscious choice over what arouses us. If women were aroused with a lover, then women would orgasm reliably every time, just as men do. Female orgasm would not be a mystery, or a male turn-on and no one would talk about it. The different ways in which women are observed responding with a lover are clearly a result of conscious behaviours rather than subconscious sexual responses.

V   Sexologists need to challenge what they are told

On an on-going basis, I ask sexologists, medical professionals, sex workers, gay men, lesbians, heterosexuals and anyone else, who might be assumed to be interested in the topic, to comment on my articles and quotes. Very few people comment, especially women. Some women get angry and defensive but they have nothing constructive to say. Some men think sex is always a topic that should be turned into a smutty joke. Most men make superficial comments. Some are supportive of the discussion. But very few can ever contribute in a meaningful way. Given the lack of sex education, everyone suffers from ignorance, embarrassment and a lack of confidence.

Why do we have so little sex education? Effectively we have voluntary censorship over the facts because so many people make money out of the fantasy view of sex. The political advantages for women, who support or condone the male view of female sexuality, are huge. A woman has nothing to gain by being honest.[41] Any woman, who is honest, is a threat to the many women worldwide who make money out of men's sexual needs. We lack experience in talking about sex. We do not know where to start. We lack facts and explanations. We have no means of informing ourselves.

We have the idea that scientific method is defined by scientists. Foremost, we assume (incorrectly) that sexologists accept the research work that has been done. Many people, such as agony aunts and journalists in popular magazines, pronounce on sexuality without having any relevant qualifications in sexology. Such information is never challenged because of the embarrassment and lack of certainty. No one knows any better. We are left to decide for ourselves what new information we will believe on the topic.

It is a nonsense to suggest that scientists can discover something that generations of couples have missed. This is a basic misunderstanding of sex research. We cannot discover something new about an instinctive response that has evolved over millions of years (from before homo sapiens). We can only give explanations for those responses. Given women's universal silence on sexual topics, men have defined their sexuality for them. Our universal sexual ignorance is due to pitiful sex education in every society.

In truth, to be an expert in sexuality one needs to have assimilated decades of experience of human nature and a long-term sexual relationship. One needs to have explored sex play. One needs to be an objective observer. One needs to be responsive, to know what arousal and orgasm feel like. One needs to be familiar with the research findings that give women a voice. One needs to be devoid of political bias and emotional prejudices.

41

References

[1] The only way to understand how nature works is to look at it and then use logic and reason to understand and explain what you see. Newton was one of the first to interrogate Nature using the principles of what we now call the 'scientific method'. In other words he observed the world, came up with theories to explain what he saw, then tested them with experiments to see if he was right. The power of this approach is that it aims to remove preconceived ideas and in doing so deliver a more accurate description of the natural world. (Professor Brian Cox)

[2] The possibility of reconciling the different sexual interests and capacities of females and males, the possibility of working out sexual adjustments in marriage, and the possibility of adjusting social concepts to allow for these differences between females and males, will depend upon our willingness to accept the realities which the available data seem to indicate. (Alfred Kinsey)

[3] I faked orgasms continuously through my marriage, but I didn't do that as a conscious malicious deception. I simply didn't know what an orgasm was – I thought it was when you felt really terrific and in love and surrendering and what not – like a 'climax' of feeling. ... And even now I'll fake an orgasm just to get the whole thing over with... (Shere Hite)

[4] Many females, of course, report that they are offended by portrayals of sexual action ... most females are indifferent or antagonistic to the existence of such material because it means nothing to them erotically. (Alfred Kinsey)

[5] Most of the books I have read are not very revealing. They don't answer the important questions. ... At our age (I am eighteen years old – almost nineteen) we really are in the dark about sex. (Shere Hite)

[6] ... even those females who are most responsive in their sexual relations might not choose to have coitus as often as their spouses want it. (Alfred Kinsey)

[7] The frequencies of orgasm ... had stayed more or less on a level from the youngest to the oldest age group. The median females in the active sample had averaged one orgasm in two weeks (0.5 per week) ... (Alfred Kinsey)

[8] If women know how to have orgasms, why don't they use this knowledge during sex with men? (Shere Hite)

[9] This is my first sexual relationship. I am eighteen – almost nineteen. I must say that I had expected much more. ... When I am having sex, I don't really feel anything. This I don't understand. I really thought that I would be able to feel his penis in me but I usually don't. (Shere Hite)

[10] I wish I could be told sometimes in the middle of the day or in bed at night, "Lie down, relax, enjoy; I'm going to give you head for an hour." (Shere Hite)

[11] For example, men found anal sexual behaviors (including anal sex, anal toys, and anal fingering) more appealing than women. The same was true for oral sex (both giving and receiving), watching a partner undress, and watching a partner masturbate. (Yella Hewings-Martin)

[12] A good many females ... contribute little or nothing ... based in part, on the theory that the male is normally so aroused that he does not need additional physical stimulation ... based in part on the theory that in a culture which considers that sex should always be associated with romanticism and gallantry, it becomes the duty of the male to provide for the pleasure of the female. (Alfred Kinsey)

[13]Many men have a completely genital approach to sex. Sex play is not play to them, but a series of mechanical manoeuvres to get the woman ready for what they really want. (Shere Hite)

[14]… the idea has been widely accepted that the effectiveness of a sexual relationship must depend primarily upon the skill and the art of the male partner in physically stimulating the female. (Alfred Kinsey)

[15]Female sexuality has been seen essentially as a response to male sexuality and intercourse. There has rarely been any acknowledgement that female sexuality might have a complex nature of its own which would be more than just the logical counterpart to (what we think of as) male sexuality. (Shere Hite)

[16]… sexual response is primarily a function of the nervous system. (Alfred Kinsey)

[17]For most males, whether single or married, there are ever-present erotic stimuli, and sexual response is regular and high. (Alfred Kinsey)

[18]We now interpret the supposed orgasms as preliminary peaks of arousal. The possibility of prolonging this sort of experience … depends on the very fact that there is no orgasm. (Alfred Kinsey)

[19]The muscular action which is involved when a female masturbates in this fashion is typical of the copulatory movements of the male (Alfred Kinsey)

[20]The penis, for example, has two roots known as crura which play an essential role in its functioning. During sexual excitation these crura become engorged with blood and contribute to erection of the penis. The clitoris, too, has two broad roots, of approximately the same size as in the male. The clitoral crura, too, become engorged with blood early in the woman's sexual excitation. (Shere Hite)

[21]The female clitoral system has a precisely analogous pair of bulbous corpora cavernosa, which similarly fill with blood during sexual excitation. (Shere Hite)

[22]No one has to learn to become tumescent, to build up neuromuscular tensions which lead to the rhythmic pelvic thrusts of coitus, or to develop any of the other responses which lead to orgasm. (Alfred Kinsey)

[23]It would also seem as if there is a definite break between sensuality (diffuse, non-focused physical feeling), and sexuality (drive toward orgasm), and that in order to have an orgasm, at least most of the time, it is necessary to think and work and concentrate toward one. (Shere Hite)

[24]Most of the men in my heterosexual career… wanted oral stimulation from me of their penis, after which they would mount me and reach their climax. After their ejaculation they would ask, "Didja come?" In general, my female lovers have taken far more creative and varied approaches to lovemaking. … The women did not act as though I was a 'masturbation machine'. (Shere Hite)

[25]… there was no correlation with frequency of orgasm: women who did not orgasm with their partner were just as likely to say they enjoyed sex as women who did. (Shere Hite)

[26]The fact that I cannot come during intercourse must mean that I do not like it, or have a shame or fear of it, even though I think I like it. I realize this but since I don't know why I am this way, I do not know how to go about overcoming it. (Shere Hite)

[27]Sex is important because when there is a feeling of … appreciation between two people – sex can make life together something special. It shows 'you mean more to me than others do'. (Shere Hite)

[28]Some women … mentioned that they have a different type of orgasm during clitoral stimulation or masturbation than during intercourse - what has often been called 'vaginal orgasm'. By this they did not mean they felt vaginal contractions, or intense clitoral or vaginal sensations, but that they felt an

intense emotional peak … accompanied by strong feelings of closeness, yearning, or exaltation. We will call this 'emotional orgasm'. (Shere Hite)

29 … even if a man has a strong physical desire for orgasm – an erection, for example – there is nothing in nature, nothing physical, that impels him to have that orgasm in a vagina. (Shere Hite)

30 The importance of masturbation for me is that it's my only source of orgasm. (Shere Hite)

31 Because males are so readily stimulated by thinking of past sexual experiences, by anticipating the opportunity to renew that experience, and by the abundant associations that they make between everyday objects and their sexual experience the average young male is constantly being aroused. The average female is not so often aroused. (Alfred Kinsey)

32 The male may be continuously stimulated by seeing the female, by engaging in erotic conversation with her, by thinking of the sexual techniques he may use, by remembering some previous sexual experience … Perhaps two-thirds of the females find little if any arousal in such psychologic stimuli. (Alfred Kinsey)

33 There is, it seems to me, an erotic continuum, of which orgasm is merely one point, one period, more intense, but qualitatively not different from the experience immediately preceding and following. (Shere Hite)

34 In short, the only real difference between men's and women's erections is that men's are on the outside of their bodies, while women's are on the inside. (Shere Hite)

35 It is impossible to believe that any male would ever be unconscious of the fact that he was aroused sexually, even if he did not have a penis to bear testimony to that effect… (Alfred Kinsey)

36 I wish making love were more sensuous touching and less direct genital activity. (Shere Hite)

37 … with my present female lover … she and I spend anywhere from two hours to six hours in caressing, touching, cuddling, hugging, lip kissing, deep kissing and intimate conversation before, in-between, and after sex, lying in bed. This is very important! (Shere Hite)

38 If you want a good orgasm, you can masturbate. The whole reason you make love with someone is to share the closeness and warmth of making love, of giving pleasure, of appreciating each other's bodies … (Shere Hite)

39 I used to (fake), because my partner was comparing me to another woman he was sleeping with. He made me feel terrible with descriptions of how she went into a screaming orgasm before he even entered her. (Shere Hite)

40 … the different position and the closeness of the partner prevent a successful masturbating technique. (Shere Hite)

41 I can see no way sex is political, unless you mean the way that women have sex with their husbands if they'll do this or that for them. I don't believe that's right, but I can't say I don't do the same kind of thing with my husband sometimes. (Shere Hite)

www.ingramcontent.com/pod-product-compliance
Lightning Source LLC
Chambersburg PA
CBHW060542030426
42337CB00021B/4401